Her No, MY NEVER

PUNIT M CHUDHARI

BlueRose ONE.com
Stories Matter
NewDelhi • London

BLUEROSE PUBLISHERS
India | U.K.

BlueRose ONE.com
Stories Matter
NewDelhi • London

For permissions requests or inquiries regarding this publication, please contact:

BLUEROSE PUBLISHERS
www.BlueRoseONE.com
info@bluerosepublishers.com
+91 8882 898 898
+4407342408967

ISBN: 978-93-7018-943-0

Cover design: Yash Singhal
Typesetting: Namrata Saini

First Edition: April 2025

About the Author

Punit Munnaji Chudhari

Punit Munnaji Chudhari is a young poet, entrepreneur, and content writer, currently studying in 12th grade at Sanjo Convent School, Gondpipri. He started his entrepreneurial journey at 14, first in online marketing and later launching Purglow, a candle and Polaroid business in 2024.

His writing journey began with nature poetry, but love soon became his greatest muse. Experiencing one-sided love, he turned his emotions into poetry, making his work deeply real and relatable. He believes love has no age and wants to give a voice to one-sided lovers, showing they are not alone.

Beyond writing, Punit excels in content creation, debating, and performing arts. He values freedom over rigid goals, following only his heart's path. His book is a reflection of raw emotions, and he hopes readers feel every word, relate to the pain and love, and share it with those who need it most.

Dear Readers,

Don't just read–feel every word, every verse, every letter. Step into the shoes of a one-sided lover. Live their emotions, understand their pain. Until you truly feel the poetry, don't turn the page. Let it sink into your heart first... then move forward. And while reading, you can listen your favourite love song {must}.

– Punit Chudhari

To the girl who inspired this story,
To the pain that became my strength,
And to the love that shaped me into
Who I am today.

This book is dedicated to all
The one - sided lovers,
To those who gathered courage or who dared to confess,
And to those who buried their feelings deep,
To the unspoken words,
the unheard stories,
And the dreams that stayed within.
This is for the hearts that loved,
Even without being loved in return.

My Handwritten proposal to Her,

To,

Charming Girl,

Let me take you back to June 27,202X. That was the day I saved a video on snapchat - it was the first time I laid eyes on you and realised I was starting to like you. At first, I thought it was just an attraction or crush, but as time went on, I slowly - slowly began to fall in love with you. How did it happen ......? Let me tell you, many people share eye contact and heartfelt smile with me, but whenever our eyes meet, and you give me that beautiful smile - IDK - It feels so damn good!! I can't put into words the happiness and the emotions I feel in those moments. It all started with that magical eye contact and smile with you. From then on, I fell in love with you!! Every poetry I'V written since December has been for you. I could write an entire book about you - your beauty, your smile, and the way your eyes speak to me. I want to say so much more in this letter, but I think it's better if I propose to you in my poetic way;

Will you be my swan ...?

Will you be my reason to write love poetries ....?

I know I cannot match your beauty or vibe, but I will love you in a thousand way, that no one can!!

{Being a poet}

I hope I can express my feelings to you.

At the end, I just want to say, I Love You ...!!, Do You ....??. If it's no, then I'll wait for you from months to years.

- *I have never read any kind of Fictional stories; can we be the stories ....?*
- *A smile on my lips, glow in my eyes, blush on my cheeks, and relief in my heart. Is the way how I react, after having a short Eye contact with you ....!!*
- *I always got my Eyes on you!*

Punit Chudhari

she always gave me beautiful eye contact.
She used to gift me heartfelt smiles,
and through those eye contacts,
Her Eyes conveyed unspoken words.
She felt like my biggest supporter.
In the end, she gave me hope,
and I started to feel this as love.
She made me blush, and that's
how I fell in love with her.
But sadly,
she didn't feel the same.

I am in a bond were,
She can't Love me and,
I can't hate her.

Why should I take the picture of Moon,
When,
In my heart there is already a Moon,
i.e., You!!!!!!

Born to write Thousands
Poetries on her,
But forced to write for,
Someone who doesn't care.

Someone asked,
Who inspired you to write ....?
And I replied,
"Her Eyes"

Today,

I met her unexpectedly,
And as a one-sided lover,
I could not sleep at night,
Just thinking about her.

She will find a face,
Better than me but,
Not the impatient heart,
That is waiting for,
Her love.

From,
An immature attraction,
To unconditional one - sided love,
Yet still,
My heart take care,
Of a room
Named, 'First Love'.

She is like angel,
That she came from the Paradise,
With fullness of sugary bliss,
Inside in her cute eyes.

Oh,
That, ‘Delight trap’,
Caught my inner self,
That was bound by,
Its inner self – affection.

Every time I see you,
I just fall more in love with you,
As you are my love weakness,
That no one can take from my life.

Someone asked me,
What do you want,
On your birthday....?
I replied,
'That angle who is sparkling
In my Eyes.'

Her smile is the,
Best expensive therapy,
That one - sided lover,
Could have.

- Small scene shot on

6th Feb 202X

For me, this day will always be unforgettable. That morning, she danced on stage in a saree, and my eyes couldn't see anyone but her. Among the entire group, only she was sparkling in my vision. Her dance lasted just a few minutes, but I have engraved it in my memory forever. My heart whispered–I could watch her dance for a lifetime. That moment brought a heartfelt smile to my face, and I felt a soft blush warming my cheeks.

After the program, I desperately wanted a photo with her. With the help of a few friends from her class, I gathered the courage to ask. And to my surprise, she agreed instantly. I still don't understand how or why–especially after being rejected just 26 days ago. Was it as a friend? Or as something more? I don't know. But that moment meant the world to me.

As a small gift, I had prepared a candle Bouquet for her. I had woken up suddenly at 3:30 a.m. that morning just to complete it. I didn't want to give her something unfinished. I watched her from the corner of the veranda, making sure she didn't notice my stolen glances.

That photo–our only photo–remains hidden in my private album. Every night before sleeping and every morning after waking up, I open it. I look at it, reliving that moment, feeling lucky that even after rejection, I got to capture that one frame with her. A frame that holds a thousand emotions–love, longing, and a silent wish that time could freeze.

Someone said,
All young needs body,
But, No!!
I just need 'Her Eyes',
To deep dive.

My Muse,
You are the Honeybee,
Let me become the,
Honeycomb,
So, you can pulse your love,
Into the chambers of my,
Heart comb.

- My thought before proposing her,

That,
What if I had proposed to her...?
What if I had spoken the words,
trapped in my heart?

I said,
Maybe our story would,
have been the cutest.
She's an introvert, quiet;
I'm the extrovert,
loud-But fear holds me back.
a silent barrier I cannot crack.

What if she says no?
What if I lose?
So, I stay lost in the 'what inner feelings and scenario'
I choose.
I don't know how to propose to her,
Don't have the courage,
nor the perfect words.
But as a poet,
I find my way-Through verses,
I speak what my heart couldn't say.
I write poetry for her,
hoping she'll reply,

A proposal through my lines,
under the open sky.
The time hasn't ended:
hope still blooms,
We can still start our cutest relationship soon.
I'm just waiting for that one moment,
When she'll gather the courage,
her heart's true sentiment.
The time hasn't ended:
hope still stays,
We can start our cutest relationship,
in countless ways.......

Ohh Cherished,
My Love will end,
Only when,
My Life meets its end.

Being with her,
Was not an Illusion,
It was my Conscious thought.

When I go to the bed,
And try to close my eyes,
I could not watch darkness,
But,
Her smile,
Her eye contact,
Her face,
And my life with her.

They asked,
Which thing would you choose,
To watch forever......?
I replied,
'Her Eyes'.

If I would feel the pain,
After my death,
The flame of wood,
Will not be much more than,
The living eye contact with her.

They said,
Don't beg Infront of her.
Then I replied,
You are saying about begging......?
I am ready to bow down,
Before her,
Ready to touch,
Her sweet feet Infront of lakhs, even
Crores of people,
Ready to kiss her feet forever.
And wash them with my
Happy tears, showcasing like pearls.
If God told me,
'You will live forever in
Heaven, where no one will be
There to disturb you,'
Then right now,
I am ready to die....
And you are talking about begging......?

Someone asked me,
How much do you love her...?
So, I just replied,
As much as stars in the sky,
As deep as the pacific endless ride,
As vast as the milky way's bright array,
As countless as the plants that
Blankets on earth,
So is my love for her,
Infinite and unmeasured.

She said to me,
Leave the love that you are,
Giving to me,
You deserve a lot better than me......
Then I replied,
How can I give the shower of love,
To anyone, that I'm giving to you....?
How can I close the love energy that,
You are transferring in my bloom of heart......?
How can I stop the unconditional heart,
That is only beating for you...?
How can I erase the ballon of future,
That I made for you in my dreams....?
Even I'll be 80, Still my heart will love you,
Like when I was 14,
So, my wave of love,
And unlovable heart,
Don't see anyone better than you,
And they don't want to.........

Someone said to me,
You are in teenage years,
It is only a physical attraction,
Not a love....
Then I replied,
Attraction is for few days,
But my love is for decades to centuries...
From the first thought in the morning,
To the last thought at night,
She is always in my mind....
Even in my dreams, she appears so near,
Bridging the gap of, Distance with every tear....
Even when she is not around me,
I see her in every person......
My eyes are always searching for her,
Every word I speak,
Every step I take, Is a quite whisper,
Calling her name....
My mind is detaching from her, But,
The nature is attaching us......
I am imagining myself with her,
After leaving this world.

To,

My illusion (Her)

My darl!!! I am sharing with you my delulu!!... It will be an imaginary world. I know in this life; we cannot be in a relationship together. It should not happen, but no one can predict destiny.

In my delulu, I will build a house made of flowers. In the backyard, there will be a garden filled with flowers, squirrels, birds, and rabbits. We will make a lake near our garden, where two swans will be there, representing us. And the house will be far, far away from the world. It will be in a forest where everything will be organic, where only we both will live. No one will be there to disturb us. The open sky will be filled with the sweetness of love, and the air will carry the fragrance of flowers.

Near our house, we will make a large farm where we will grow organic fruits and vegetables. For work, we will adopt some animals from the jungle. Life will be pure, filled with endless love. We will merge together into nature, and I will be there as a worker for you. You will be a goddess to me.

Every morning and evening, I will wash your feet with my happy tears mixed with honey. I will look into your eyes—the same eyes that made me fall in love with you forever. I know this will never be real, but I wish that in the next universe, in the next parallel life, we will merge together.

It can be possible even in this life, but you need to say yes, and I will be ready to leave my career, my life—just to be there for you. No worries, no tensions. We will just buy a piece of land and live.

I hope I could deliver my imagination to you.

- your one side lover

Someone said,
'What can be the
sweetest thing ever....?'
and I just replied,
"Her voice".

In English we say,
"You are beautiful,
Your eyes are so lovely."
But in poetry,
Let me become,
the mirror,
so, I can see you always,
holding your image,
in my heart forever.
Let me become,
The rays of the moon,
So, I can gently touch your beauty,
And feel its warmth.
Let me become,
The stars in the night sky,
Shining high in bright sky.
Whenever you pass by,
I will bright high.

They said,
What do you get when you love her...?
Then I replied,
I will never get tired,
By loving her,
Loving her is my,
Happiness....
Loving her endlessly,
Brings happiness no,
Other moments can......!!
And I know the value,
Of happiness,
That I am getting,
From her my darl...!!
That happiness is,
Price less for my,
Unconditional heart...
She will never,
Understand the happiness,
That I am getting from her....

In English we say,
'No one loves me,
I am unloved by everyone'.
But I said,
For me,
Love was delusional and illusion,
That was creation of my mind.

Someone asked me,
"What do you hope from her,
If she falls in love with you...?
What will you do...?"
I replied,
I still hope that one day,
We'll gaze at the moon together,
I hope that one day, we'll sit by the riverbanks,
Sharing our love stories, For hours.
I hope that one day,
We'll travel the world, Side by side.
I dream of us watching the sunset,
Wrapped in each other's warmth.
I hope that in the quiet of the night,
Our hearts will speak the, Words left unspoken.
I hope that someday, we will write our story together,
Line by line, Under the stars.
But guess what......,
Endlessly, I was just dreaming about,
These things...., I know it will be never true.

Someone asked me,
How much you can write about her…?
And I replied,
I will write to her,
So deeply in my words,
That the,
One who reads will,
Beg to see her…
Because I write,
Not in being relationship,
But I write,
Poetries for that,
One person,
Who never liked,
Me back……

When I think,
You are in my life,
But,
When I see,
You,
Belong to someone else.

The art of eye contact,

Sometimes I think,
Two beautiful stars,
Of the sky,
Where pasted instead,
Of her eyes.....!!
The real house for the stars,
Where her eyes, but they just
Misplaced, scattered in the heavens....
Eyes were sparkling like, The pearl of the glory.
Eyes were transferring,
The feelings, emotions and
Some unsaid words that,
Mouth couldn't express...!!
The eye contact was, For a few seconds but,
Every moment became, Unforgettable for my soul!!
By seeing her eyes, my lips, started to smile,
Along with her eyes. Her eyes are giving,
The peace of sweetness....

They said,
She hates you...
Then also why you love her...?
I replied,
I am a fool who finds love, In Her hate.
I am a fool who loves, Her hate.
I don't see her hate; I just see that at least she,
Thinks about me. The more she hates,
The more my love, Increases...!
As it's said,
I fall in love with, Everything about her.
Her smile, Her gaze, Her hate, Her silence,
Her ignorance.
Just everything...!
Even her last words of, Conversation feels better,
Than watching a sunset,
Or talking with nature, just no words......!!
Even if her hate, Becomes my shadow,
I'll walk in its warmth,
For its part of her, and that's all I need......

In English we say,
"ugly",
But in poetry,
I find myself ugly,
When I fall in love with her.
Thinking she doesn't,
Deserve me,
Someone like me.
She's so damned, Beautifull......!!!!
I feel I can never match,
Her perfection.
I find myself even uglier,
When she rejects me,
I look into the mirror,
Searching for flaws.
Not just on my face,
But deep within,
Every imperfection, Screams louder,
Making me see the ugliness,
I never knew existed.

In English, we say,
"I never cried for her,
From months to years' "
But in poetry,
After my death,
My ashes,
Will show the,
Tears of mine,
That I never cried,
For her,
That tears,
Will flow and dissolve easily,
In water.........
And so,
For forever,
It will flow.

In English we say,
She wears a saree.
But in poetry, we say...
She is gorgeous, beautiful, cute,
And divine in her school dress...
But in a saree,
Words fail me.
Diamonds, rubies, gold, -
All pale in front of her saree.
A thousand times I watch her,
Each time with different eyes.
And yet,
Every sight reveals,
Just an incomplete shine of her.
If poetry had a shape,
It would be the folds of her
Saree, moving softly,
Telling a new verse with
Every step.
She walks.

To,

The moon I could never reach.

In school, I did everything I could just to watch you, to steal a glance, to stare at you from a distance. I don't know why, but watching you made me feel completely at peace. And whenever you passed by my side, my heart would start beating faster, my body would shiver, and those who knew about my love for you—my friends—would take my name in front of you. I would blush, lower my gaze, and smile to myself.

I still remember standing near the cycle stand in the early morning, watching you from a corner of the veranda, as if I was taking devotion of you. During the morning assembly, while everyone prayed, I was staring at you, whispering your name like a silent chant. Whenever I gave a speech or read something on stage, I remember how, in every outside assembly, we would secretly laugh, stealing glances at each other. It was our silent conversation. It was unforgettable.

I often found silly excuses to visit your class—not for any real reason, but just to watch you, to feel the warmth of your eyes. And whenever we crossed paths, we always exchanged a smile and an eye contact, as if it was something we were meant to do, something we could never skip.

I remember standing near your cycle, touching it softly, feeling as if I was touching a part of you.

These small moments, these unnoticed gestures, were my world.

But I never knew... the smile you gave me; you gave to others too.

And maybe that's what started it all—the love that grew silently, the love that never stopped.

My muse...!!

forever.

Punit Chudhari

I am an anglerfish,
Lost in the deep,
She is the light I could never keep.
Before I could reach,
Before I could touch,
The glow fades...
And I die.

After my death,
From my body,
No white smoky soul,
Will come,
Instead,
Her eye contact,
Her ignorance,
Her memories,
Her hate,
Her actions,
Her burning saree,
Only her,
Will come...

After my death,
Loudly,
Every wood flame,
Will scream,
After burning my body,
From that flame,
People will only find,
Her and her eyes,
That are merged,
With my body.

After my death,
Still,
My photo,
My ashes,
My air,
My flowers,
My rabbits,
My diary,
My poetry,
My handwritten letters,
Everything of mine,
Will scream loud,
With her name,
And will search for her.

Moving on doesn't mean you never loved her.

It's human nature to heal and grow. You should move on when your heart- not your pain- tells you it's time. Your life is valuable, not just for you, but for your family and friends. It will take time, so don't force it. One day, your heart will whisper that person no longer holds you back, and that's when you should let go. Falling in love again doesn't erase your first love- it simply means you're choosing to live, to embrace new beginnings without guilt or hesitation.

I traced her face in my mind,
a thousand times,
as if knowing every curve would bring her closer.
But she never looked at me,
The way I looked at her.
And my love remained an unseen painting,
On a blank canvas.

From my last breath,
The air will know,
That,
My breath leaves,
Her incomplete memories,
In the air,
That will spread,
For forever.

- Small scene shot on

8 Feb 202X

It was totally unexpected–something I could never imagine, not even in my dreams. In the morning, she unfollowed me on Instagram and removed me from her follower list.

When I opened her account and saw this, I was completely blank, unable to think straight. A few minutes later, she blocked me. My mind froze–I just sat in the corner of my room, staring at nothing, lost in thoughts of her. She also blocked me on Snapchat and Instagram. I know someone, maybe her sister, manipulated her because she was never like this. She was always so supportive, so different from other girls. But what hurt me the most was that she knew–she knew that blocking me would break me, yet she still did it.

I have just one question for her:

"Did you never think about how I would feel after seeing this?"

She knew it would hurt me, yet she went ahead. After that, I lost all interest in posting stories or notes on Instagram. For days, I became an offline person, still using Instagram but without sharing anything. Because every time I posted, she liked my stories–every single one of them. And her one like meant more to me than a million likes from others. Without it, Instagram felt meaningless. And then, yesterday, she replied to me on

Snapchat–cold and full of hate. It hurt. Maybe she thinks that if she ignores me, taunts me, or shows hatred, I will leave her. But she is wrong. I know she can never truly hate me because she understands my feelings. I will wait. Forever.

No matter what happens, I will always be eager–waiting for her notification, just one message from her.

She is hide in my eyes,
She is hide in my smile,
She is hide in my tears,
She is hide in my heart,
She is hide in my poetries,
She is hide in my handwritten letters,
But,
In her life,
I don't exist anywhere.

She is like the ocean,
Where her eyes,
Are deep as Pacific Ocean,
Where I want to live.

To,

My muse.

How lovely you are while practicing dance. I never knew that, like your eyes, your dance steps would burn my heart. Whenever I saw, you were practicing dance, I was happily watching your every step while sitting under a tree.

I was dreaming that if we merged together, we would be the best couple duo—where I would sing your favourite songs, and you would dance in front of my eyes. Watching you, I would remember every lyric of every song you love.

You would dance in the field of nature, in the midst of dandelion flowers, while I sat in the shadow of a tree. The animals and birds would be our audience, making chaotic sounds and clapping for us.

With me, the birds would sing in a beautiful way, and from heaven, all the gods would watch your dance. Seeing you, they would shower sweet flowers and colours upon you.

I know my voice may not match your every dance step, but I hope you would still like it when I sing. How peaceful it would be... I know it will never come true on this planet.

That's why, if you are ready, we will create our own planet—one filled with our creations, where no one will disturb us, only you and me.

Watching your dance steps with those burning eyes sets my heart on fire. I know I may sound like a madman, but I have become one—because of your eyes.

Punit

In English,
We say, "Let Her Go",
But in poetry,
She is the flowing wind,
I could never hold in my hands,
She follows her own way of love,
Her own path,
She is everywhere,
Yet never with me.
I was just a fool,
Trying to build cage,
Of love to keep her close,
But how can I confine,
Someone who is my whole world ?
How can I hide the one who is my life ?

So, I bow to her choice,
I let her go,
To live, to live, to love, to be free

If courage were a language.
I could speak,
I'd tell her how her eyes,
Make my world unique.

To,

Her Supportive Kindness,

Today, I want to share my excitement when I saw your notification on my mobile. Our love story started with that eye contact and then with those Instagram and Snapchat notifications.

Many of my Instagram followers like my stories, posts, reels, and notes, but whenever you like them, my heart fills with gallons of happiness. The thing is, you genuinely like my content and poetry. Your one notification makes my day perfect. And if you don't like my story, I start wondering—what's wrong? What have I posted?

It might be a small thing for you, but for me, it matters a lot. And do you know why I always post my poetry and philosophy on social media? Because I know you're a little bit of an old soul, someone who loves poetry, literature, art, and philosophy.

I will never forget our English chats, where I always made grammar mistakes. Our conversations would end after just a few sentences, but still, I loved talking to you.

I hope I could make you understand my story of social media—because, in the end, you were one of the reasons I fell in love with you.

Punit

If pearls could have a voice,
They would sound just like hears-
Soft, rare, and priceless.

They asked,
What will you choose...?
Moon or stars,
I replied,
"Her eyes".

Her lips had the power to heal,
But they never called my name.
I kept searching for hidden feelings,
But she never felt the same.

Her name is just a word,
But for me,
It's a whole world.
I carved it on my heart,
But she never even wrote,
Mine in her diary.

She smiled at the world,
Like she was smiling on me,
But,
I felt it was different for me.
But,
it was not.

Her voice wasn't just sound,
It was a melody I wanted to get lost in.
But I was just an audience,
Never ever the song.

To,

Her Love...

Sometimes, I wonder if we were ever meant to be, or if I was just destined to love you from afar, like a silent prayer that never reaches the heavens. People tell me, "Move on. There are better things waiting for you. You deserve someone who chooses you, someone who sees your worth." They speak as if love is a choice, as if the heart listens to reason. But what they don't understand is—I don't want to move on.

Do they know what it feels like to fear their own healing? To dread the day when the heart stops aching, not because it has found peace, but because it has grown numb? My biggest fear isn't that I'll stay stuck in this love—it's that one day, I might stop loving you. That your face will blur in my memories, that your name will no longer bring a storm in my chest, and that I will look at another girl the way I once looked at you.

But how could I? How could I ever see anyone else when my eyes have memorized only you? The world might call others beautiful, but to me, they are shadows—pale; and lifeless in front of you. You are the only one who holds the colour of my world. No matter how many faces I pass by, yours is the only one I search for, the only one that lingers in my mind when I close my eyes.

I have tried. I have tried to see someone else, to let go, to unlove you. But the moment I do, your *eyes flash before me, stopping me in my tracks, pulling me back into the gravity of this one-sided love. I have lost count of how many times I have stood at the edge of moving on, only to take a step back—because leaving you behind feels like losing a part of myself.*

And if waiting for you is the only way I can love you, then tell me—how long should I wait? Give me a number, a deadline, a limit. Let me know how many more sunrises I must witness alone, how many more nights I must write unsent letters, how many more years I must carry this love in silence. Because walking away may be easy, but loving you, even if it breaks me, is something I cannot stop doing.

- Punit Chudhari

She cried,
And the world paused,
But not for me.
Her tears fell like poetry,
Yet I was never the reason,
Behind.

She never hurt me,
Never ignored me,
Never pushed me away.
She was kind,
And that was the worst part-
Because kindness kept my hope alive,
When love was never there.

I whispered your name a thousand times,
But it never echoed back.
I wrote it beside mine in the air,
But the wind refused to carry it.
Maybe even the universe knew,
Some names were never meant,
To belong together.

I built a home inside my heart,
Furnished it with your laughter,
Lit it up with your eyes,
But you never moved in.
Now, I live alone in a place,
That was never meant for just one.

You walked away,
But my love didn't follow.
It stayed,
Rooted deep in my chest,
Growing like an unwanted tree,
That no one ever planted.

Her eyes told a thousand stories,
But none had my name.
I searched for myself in her gaze,
Only to find that I was just another face,
Passing through the pages of her life.

To,

Sweetheart.

Tell me, why must you be the reason behind my pain? I am losing myself in your love, waiting for the day when you will say, "Yes, I love you too." My life has started to resemble Majnu from Laila Majnu—where I exist only to wait for you.

" इंतज़ार, इंतज़ार सिर्फ एक लंबा सा इंतज़ार,
सामने खड़ी है, फिर भी एक लंबा सा इंतजार"

Since the day I confessed, my health has been failing. Every time I take a bite of food, your face appears before my eyes, your memories hit me like waves, and I am left standing with an empty stomach. It's not that I don't want to eat—it's that my hunger has been replaced by the ache of your love and your silence.

I have developed strange habits—murmuring to myself, constantly creating Shayaris and poetry, thinking of you, imagining you beside me. My mother thinks I am going mad, but she doesn't understand—I am not mad, I am just drowning in love. Every moment, I wonder how to make you understand the depth of my feelings.

I feel like I am dying every day, every minute. I have lost interest in everything—my passions, my career, even the fame I once thought mattered. What is the use of being a poet when all my words were meant for you? I never wanted to be a writer;

I just wanted to write about you. And now, I don't even know why I exist anymore.

I don't believe in God, but still, I find myself praying to every deity, hoping that maybe one of them will bring you to me. I don't know where else to beg for you. People read my poetry and think I am insane—but I am not. It is love that has turned me into this.

Tell me, how much longer should I wait for you? How many more days should I endure this slow death? I am still here, waiting.

My darling...

- Punit Chudhari

Imagine,
What if she comes near you and says yes?
I replied,
At that moment, I would cry and laugh together,
My voice would tremble, words slipping away,
Like a waterfall held back for two years,
Finally breaking free.
Her worries would be mine to carry,
Her happiness, my only prayer.
I would take the kohl from her eyes,
And mix it into mine forever.
If she stood in the rain and wished for sunshine,
I would beg the sun to shine for her,
Or swallow the monsoon just to keep her dry.
I would write our names on the moon,
So even in darkness, we glow together.
I would hold her hand, not just for today,
But for every lifetime we are given.
From that day on, she would be mine,
And I, forever hers.

They said,
Have some self - respect......
And I replied,
For her,
I'm ready to be a mad person,
Who will dance,
Sing a song, Laugh like a mad,
Talk like a child, Live like a beggar,
Ready to do ,whatever she says,
Infront of her,
I am just, The dust of her sandal.
I am ready, to be a shameless person,
Infront of billons of peoples.
Ready to leave, My ego and attitude,
For her, I am urging,
To worship like a devotee,
For me she is just a goddess.
For me,
I don't care about,
My self – respect.

The eyes that teach me to love her,
How that eyes can,
Hate her....?
And,
She wants that Eyes,
To hate her,
But how....?

This is how one-sided love looks like,

I was loving her,
Unconditionally,
But,
She was waiting for,
My suicide and
My death.
And,
I'm mad,
Who is ready,
To accept it....!!

Every night, I close my eyes...
not to sleep, but to meet her again.
In my dreams,
we sit on a quiet bench,
legs dipped in pearl-warm water...
fishes dancing, dolphins diving,
flowers falling around us like whispers of love.
The sun sets like never before,
watching over our talks...
our unspoken confessions.
The cold waves shivers at our talk...
I tell her how I fell in love,
how every step I took was for her...
and she listens,
her silence speaking louder than words.
I hold her hands,
tears slipping through my fingers...
crying unconditionally,
and she loves me back—finally.

Our talks never end,
our love feels eternal,
she chooses me...
But suddenly...
the alarm rings.
I wake up, staring at the ceiling,

heart still lost in that dream.
Another morning without her,
another day waiting for the night...
to meet her again.

To,

Her hate.

I don't understand—is loving someone unconditionally wrong? I don't know why you're finding hate in my love. For many years, I've known you, but I never imagined you had a hateful side. I've tried my best to impress you and show you my infinite love, but you see it as hate. Every step I take toward you; you interpret as hate and ignorance. I never knew that one day you would become like an Instagram user in my account—I never dreamed you would stop giving me eye contact and a heartfelt smile.

If loving someone unconditionally results in hate from them, then from this moment on, I'll stop loving anyone. Yet, just a few days ago, you were supporting me in every action and success. What happened after I proposed to you that made you hate me? Before, you were so kind, but now you speak so rudely to me. I know someone must have manipulated you to give me these hateful comments, but I don't know how to respond with hate or taunts. The same eyes that made me fall in love with you are now making me hate myself—but how can I hate you when I love you unconditionally?

Most of the time, I've said sorry to you from the bottom of my heart, whether or not it was my fault, because I wanted our bond to be unbreakable. Over time, you started seeing my apologies as begging. In front of you, I'm an extrovert, but because of these situations, I'm slowly closing my door, not talking much, avoiding people, losing interest in everything, and becoming an introvert in both mind and speech. Your hate is shaping me into a very different person. Now, in my letters and poetries, I show you as a hateful person with a bad mentality, but I don't want to portray you like this—it's just what I'm seeing.

After feeling your hate, I'm like a living corpse—a body without a soul—begging for your love. Please, give me one last chance. I just want to talk to you in private for a few hours so I can share my feelings and emotions with you. We can sit on an old bench in a garden and clear up all our misunderstandings.

And the photo I took with you was unforgettable. I don't know why you agreed to that photo, but I'm lucky to have taken one with you. Now you might not be with me, but our photo is still in my private album, stored forever. Whenever I feel lonely, I open that album and see our photo. Every time I look at it, my heart overflows with love. I tried my best to impress you, but you see it as hate. I was giving you love, yet each time you gave me hate. You see my goodness as badness. My intention was to make a good impression in your eyes, but it didn't happen.

I don't know how you suddenly changed your mind about my character and love, and every hateful word from you breaks my hopes. To me, *you are like the air—close enough for me to feel but impossible to hold. It's just my imagination, but how can I explain how much I want you? I want to keep you forever in front of my eyes, because I'm incomplete without you...!!*

My darU!

PUNIT

- Small scene shot on

10 Feb 202X

I never cried for her in the last two years. But today, when I saw her, I felt like I should touch her feet and just cry my heart out.

It was the first day of my final exam, and by some stroke of luck, she got the seat right next to mine, parallel to my bench. I didn't know whether to write my exam or just keep looking into her eyes until my heart felt full of love.

For a moment, I felt sad–just one seat away from her. One single seat. If only fate had been a little kinder...

But soon, I gave in to my heart. I kept stealing glances–at her eyes, her hands writing on the paper, the way her fingers moved as she scribbled. I even watched her as she cheated a little, just a tiny bit, even though she's the topper of her class. Every little action, every tiny movement–I was lost in her.

To me, she felt like a goddess sitting there. And in that moment, all I wanted was to touch her feet and just break down completely. But I couldn't.

It had been three days since I last saw her eyes, and today, I fell for them all over again. Maybe she was pretending to ignore me, but deep down, she knew everything.

I kept waiting for that one moment–when she would pass me a soft, heartwarming smile, when her eyes would meet mine with the same depth I feel for her.

For 2.5 hours, I just watched her. And those 2.5 hours felt like 2.5 minutes.

I didn't even realize how fast time flew. She was busy writing her answers, and I was just watching her.

And today–the day felt too beautiful.

But I wanted more than just looking at her–I wanted her attention, even if it was just for a second.

So, I started making funny sounds whenever the sir or ma'am left the room. I was cheating–just to get her attention. I wanted her to laugh at me, smile at me, notice me. Sometimes she did, but mostly, she ignored me.

I don't know why.

I tried everything–laughing loudly, joking with my friends, talking to the guy sitting near her, making funny gestures–just so she would look at me. Because I know, I'm a funny person. And I thought maybe, just maybe, she would notice me and smile. But she didn't.

And that hurt more than anything.

In English we say,
"I curse you "
But in poetry,
Even if she holds a knife for me,
I will never think bad about her...
never wish her pain.
But one day,
I hope she feels the same,
Loving someone who never loves her back,
Craving for someone who never even looks at her.
May she suffer the same silence,
The same ignorance, the same emptiness...
Just like I did, just like I still do.
And in that moment, when her heart aches,
When she waits for a message that never comes,
When she looks at someone the way I looked at her...
Maybe then,
she'll understand what I felt.

Everyone says,
God has a better plan for you,
just believe!!!
But, I said,
I don't need a better life,
I just need her to make it perfect.
Why should I believe in God,
when He ignored my prayers,
my devotion,
my fasts,
and my love for her?
When she was never written in my fate,
then what is the use of a God,
who never listened?

She asked,
What did you saw in me ,
That made you fall in love...?

I smiled and replied,
I saw a connection that your eyes couldn't see,
A bond beyond this life,
a thread from a past we may have forgotten,
You may not remember,
but I do.
In another time,
in another world,
we were something...
and maybe,
just maybe,
I'm still holding on to that invisible string,
hoping you'd feel it too.

She said,
I'm not even that pretty to fall in love with.

I replied,
In my eyes,
you are the ultimate truth of my life,
my purpose,
my everything.
I never fell for your outer beauty;
I fell for the depth in your eyes,
the way they speak without words.
For me,
nothing in this world holds more beauty than you.
In front of your eyes,
even the brightest stars fade.

They said,
Waiting is one of the purest forms of love.

I replied,
Maybe for those who are loved back.
But for me,
waiting is just another way,
to break myself every day, piece by piece.
How long should I wait?
From hours to decades?
I am still waiting,
knowing deep down,
she may never return.
But if love means waiting,
then I have already loved her beyond lifetimes.

She Said ,
"I don't love you I have never seen love in my eyes for uhh I juss made eye contact and gave a smile as I do too everyone!!"
I replied,
Yes,
it was my mistake...
My mistake to seal love in your pretty starlit eyes.
It was my fault to find meaning,
in the way you looked at me.
I mistook your common smile as something rare,
something just for me.
But it wasn't... It was never special to you.
It was my own heart that,
turned your gaze into poetry,
your smile into a promise.
And maybe,
it was my greatest mistake,
to love you when you never meant,
to be loved by me.

To,

Her.

I don't know whether I am sad or happy. Every day, every single moment, you kill me, and yet, somehow, you keep me alive. I find myself holding on to the smallest things—your fleeting eye contact, a hesitant smile, a moment of silence that feels like a conversation. I search for these crumbs of hope, thinking, maybe today, she will see me the way I see her. But then, reality slaps me harder than my dreams ever could.

I see you with someone else, laughing, lost in a world where I don't exist. And I want to ask you—why did you reject me? You gave me a reason, but my heart refuses to accept it. Do you ever wonder what happened to me after that day? Did you ever stop to think how rejection feels when the only thing I ever wanted was you?

I question everything now. My face—is it not good enough? Might be it is not ! My character—was there ever a flaw you saw? I stand before the mirror, not searching for beauty but for imperfections—flaws that I never cared about before, but now, they define me. I wonder, what should I change? What would make you choose me?

I regret only one thing—not confessing earlier, when my love was still soft, when it wasn't drowning in desperation. But how could I not tell you after loving you for so long? It was my duty to let you know. And yet, when you rejected me, something inside me broke in a way that no glue, no poetry, no time can ever fix.

You might think I cried a lot after you walked away. No. Not a single tear fell. It's strange, isn't it? My heart is shattered, but my eyes remain dry. Maybe because my pain is too heavy for tears to carry. Or maybe, because deep down, I still wait for you.

But tell me—if you never loved me, why did you look at me the way you did? Why did your eyes speak when your lips refused to? Did you ever ask them before rejecting me? Because I did. And they told me stories of love you never said out loud.

After that day, you stopped looking at me altogether. As if by erasing me from your vision, you could erase me from existence. But I'm still here. Still waiting. I don't expect you to love me—I have accepted that love is not a reward for patience—but I just want to know why? Why did you give me hope if you knew it was never meant to be mine?

My nights have changed since then. I sleep at 10:30 p.m., only to wake up at 2:30 a.m., staring at the ceiling, lost in thoughts of you. I try to sleep, but you refuse to leave my mind. Your voice, your smile, the way you once looked at me—all of it comes back like waves, striking me over and over.

I am not begging in front of the world, but in front of you, I am on my knees. Would you ever *choose me? I know your answer. I have known it since the day you said no. But no matter how many times you say it, a small part of me—just 8%—will always hope. And this hope % is from your birth date.*

Tell me, what should I do to belong to you? Should I change the way I look, the way I talk, the way I love? Should I rewrite myself into someone you could accept? Or am I destined to remain just a forgotten name in your past? I have tried everything—becoming better, becoming quieter, becoming invisible—yet nothing seems enough. Tell me, what more should I do? What is missing in me that makes me unworthy of you?

And after reading this letter, you need to answer all of my questions. Not because I expect a yes, not because I want to force anything upon you, but because this is the only way my heart will find a moment of peace. It is my heart's request to you. Do not leave me in silence, do not let my words disappear into nothingness. If I am not enough, tell me why. If I was never meant to be yours, then let me hear it from you one last time. But please, don't let me keep searching for answers in the dark—you are the only one who can give them to me.

Yours,

Punit Chudhari

Please, don't take any more hatred from my letters and poetries. If you do, I won't exist in this world anymore. I never wanted to paint you as a bad person in my story, but the situations are making you one. If my love still feels like a burden to you...

I hope...!!

– A Mad One-Sided Lover

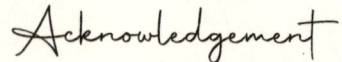

Acknowledgement

I extend my heartfelt gratitude to my grandfather for his wisdom and understanding, and to my father and mother for their unwavering support and belief in me. Your presence in my life is my greatest strength.

A special thank you to my sisters, Leena and Komal, for always standing beside me like a shadow, cheering me on in every step of my journey.

To Anushka, Sarvesh, and Tejaswini–your words, your encouragement, and your endless faith in me have been the pillars that held my poetry together. You saw the writer in me before the world did, and for that, I will always be grateful. Your support wasn't just appreciation; it was the fire that kept my words alive.

Thank you all for being a part of my story.

Follow My Account on Instagram

@HERNOMYNEVER_BOOK

Now,

I am waiting for the day you say,

'Punit, it was never one-sided... I love you too♥!!'

www.ingramcontent.com/pod-product-compliance
Lightning Source LLC
LaVergne TN
LVHW041615070526
838199LV00052B/3158
* 9 7 8 9 3 7 0 1 8 9 4 3 0 *